Test# 87702

R.L 5.7

Pts. 1.0

MOVING PEOPLE, THINGS, AND IDEAS

A HISTORY OF WATER TRAVEL

Text by Renzo Rossi

BLACKBIRCH PRESS

An imprint of Thomson Gale, a part of The Thomson Corporation

THOMSON

GALE

Detroit • New York • San Francisco • San Diego • New Haven, Conn. • Waterville, Maine • London • Munich

THOMSON
GALE

Copyright © 2004 by Andrea Dué s.r.l., Florence, Italy

Published in 2005 in North America by Thomson Gale

Conception and production: Andrea Dué s.r.l.
Text: Renzo Rossi
Translation: Erika Pauli
Illustrations: Alessandro Baldanzi, Alessandro Bartolozzi, Leonello Calvetti, Lorenzo Cecchi, Sauro Giampaia, Luigi Ieracitano, Roberto Simoni, Donato Spedaliere
Research, documentation, and layout: Luigi Ieracitano
Cutouts: Uliana Derniatina

Photo Credits: Pages 13 (top), 39: Farabolafoto; page 14: Scala Archives; page 42-43: Franco Pace

For more information, contact
Blackbirch Press
27500 Drake Rd.
Farmington Hills, MI 48331-3535
Or you can visit our Internet site at http://www.gale.com

LIBRARY OF CONGRESS CATALOGING-IN-PUBLICATION DATA

Rossi, Renzo, 1940–
    A History of Water Travel / by Renzo Rossi.
        p. cm. — (Moving people, things, and ideas)
    "Previously published with Enchanted Lion Books"—Data sheet.
    Includes bibliographical references and index.
    ISBN 1-4103-0662-3 (hardcover: alk. paper)
    1. Boats and boating—Juvenile literature. 2. Ships—Juvenile literature.
    I. Title. II. Series.

    VM150.R6275 2005
    387'.009—dc22

                                                    2004028581

Printed in the United States
10 9 8 7 6 5 4 3 2 1

Contents

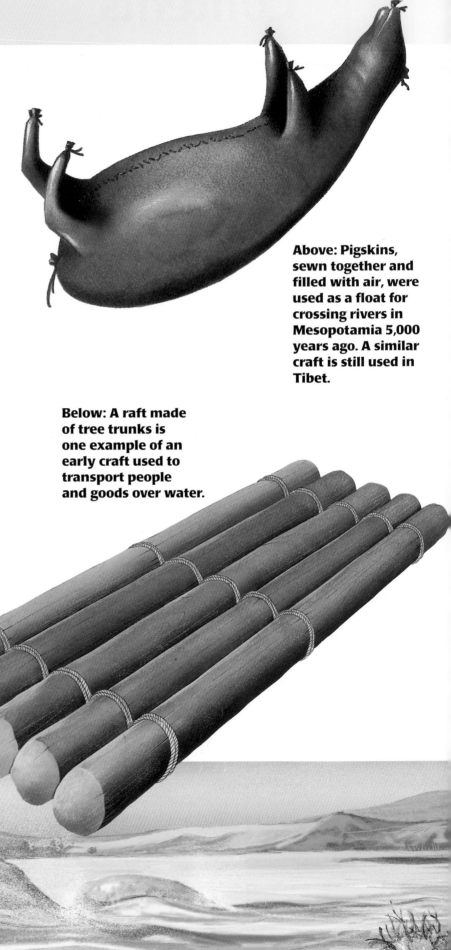

From the earliest times, people have been on the move. People traveled because they had to follow the animals that provided them with food. People also traveled out of curiosity, to explore new places.

For at least 2 million years, people explored lands by following the courses of rivers or the shores of lakes. At first, they were afraid to try to cross water. But then they realized that a tree trunk or a bundle of reed plants could float and could keep them afloat, too. This is how water travel began.

Scientists believe that people began to invent ways to cross water around the end of the Paleolithic period, tens of thousands of years ago. Though human communities at that time were scattered among five continents, people's ideas for water travel were similar from place to place. For example, scientists think that one early attempt at crossing water involved rafts made from tree trunks or bundles of reeds. Another involved filling animal skins with air and using them as floats.

Above: Pigskins, sewn together and filled with air, were used as a float for crossing rivers in Mesopotamia 5,000 years ago. A similar craft is still used in Tibet.

Below: A raft made of tree trunks is one example of an early craft used to transport people and goods over water.

Below: The first watercraft may have been a floating tree trunk.

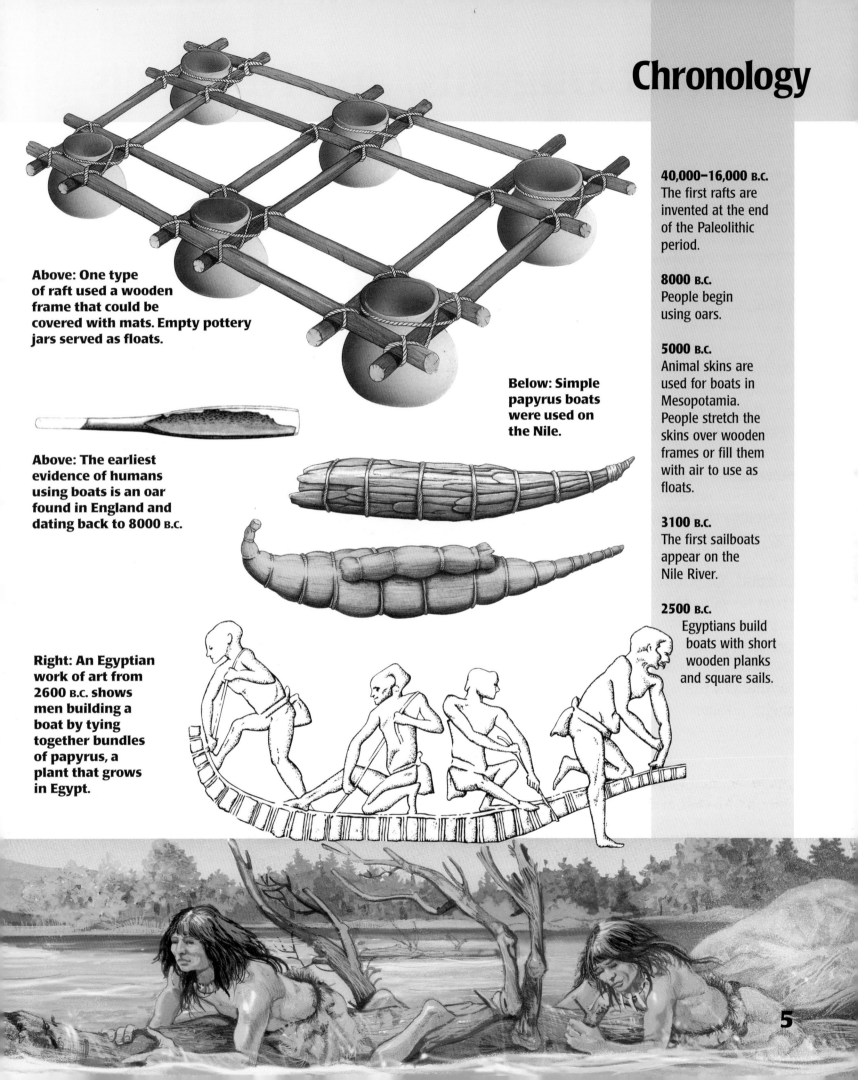

Chronology

Above: One type of raft used a wooden frame that could be covered with mats. Empty pottery jars served as floats.

Above: The earliest evidence of humans using boats is an oar found in England and dating back to 8000 B.C.

Below: Simple papyrus boats were used on the Nile.

Right: An Egyptian work of art from 2600 B.C. shows men building a boat by tying together bundles of papyrus, a plant that grows in Egypt.

40,000–16,000 B.C.
The first rafts are invented at the end of the Paleolithic period.

8000 B.C.
People begin using oars.

5000 B.C.
Animal skins are used for boats in Mesopotamia. People stretch the skins over wooden frames or fill them with air to use as floats.

3100 B.C.
The first sailboats appear on the Nile River.

2500 B.C.
Egyptians build boats with short wooden planks and square sails.

Baskets, Dugouts, and Nutshells

Some boats that were made in ancient times are still used today. For example, round boats, shaped much like the tiny toy boats children sometimes make from walnut shells, are common. Round boats have been used in many places throughout the world, including Wales, Greenland, China, and Tibet.

The paracil is a round boat used today on the rivers of southern India. It is made of buffalo skins stretched over a frame of bamboo slats. The paracil is stiff but light. Another type of round boat is the quffa (basket), used on the Tigris and Euphrates rivers. A quffa is made of woven leather strips that have been treated to resist water. It can carry as many as twenty people.

Dugouts are another type of early boat. They were made by hollowing out tree trunks. People hollowed them out by burning or chipping or scraping with stone tools. Dugouts have been used in many places throughout the world. Dugouts are common in New Zealand, Canada, Africa, and South and Central America.

Top: The quffa (above) is the round boat of Mesopotamia. The paracil (below) is the round boat of India.

Right: A gold model of an ancient Irish boat, dating to the 1st century B.C., was found in Ireland. It is believed to be a coracle or curragh. This kind of boat was made from cowhides stretched on a frame of willow branches.

Left: A small round boat, a toy made from a walnut shell, can have a toothpick mast decorated with a flag.

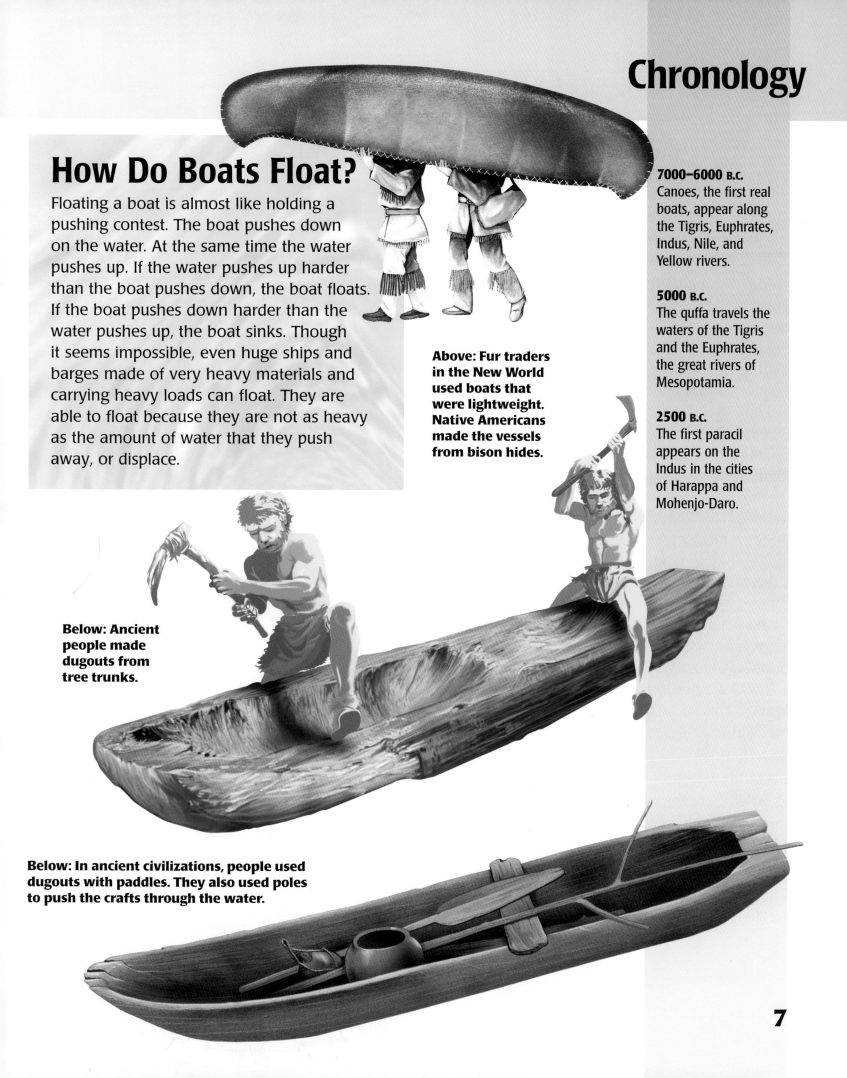

How Do Boats Float?

Floating a boat is almost like holding a pushing contest. The boat pushes down on the water. At the same time the water pushes up. If the water pushes up harder than the boat pushes down, the boat floats. If the boat pushes down harder than the water pushes up, the boat sinks. Though it seems impossible, even huge ships and barges made of very heavy materials and carrying heavy loads can float. They are able to float because they are not as heavy as the amount of water that they push away, or displace.

Above: Fur traders in the New World used boats that were lightweight. Native Americans made the vessels from bison hides.

7000–6000 B.C.
Canoes, the first real boats, appear along the Tigris, Euphrates, Indus, Nile, and Yellow rivers.

5000 B.C.
The quffa travels the waters of the Tigris and the Euphrates, the great rivers of Mesopotamia.

2500 B.C.
The first paracil appears on the Indus in the cities of Harappa and Mohenjo-Daro.

Below: Ancient people made dugouts from tree trunks.

Below: In ancient civilizations, people used dugouts with paddles. They also used poles to push the crafts through the water.

Building Boats

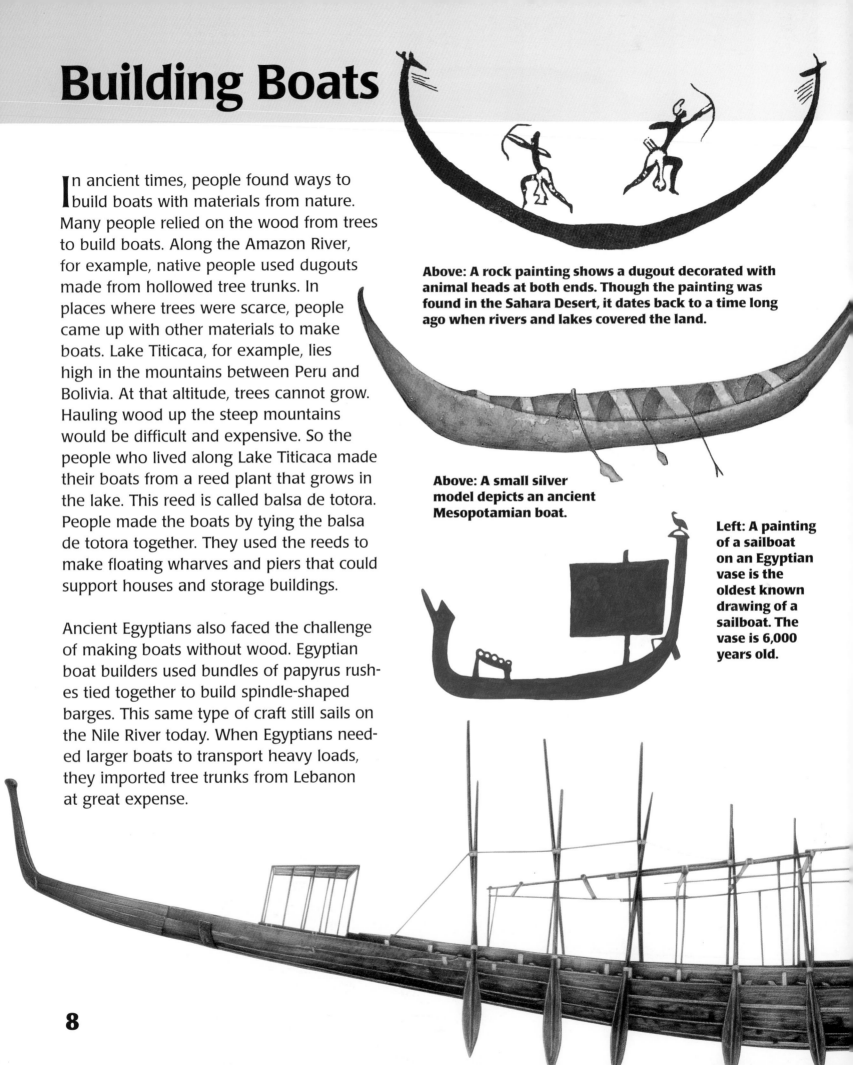

In ancient times, people found ways to build boats with materials from nature. Many people relied on the wood from trees to build boats. Along the Amazon River, for example, native people used dugouts made from hollowed tree trunks. In places where trees were scarce, people came up with other materials to make boats. Lake Titicaca, for example, lies high in the mountains between Peru and Bolivia. At that altitude, trees cannot grow. Hauling wood up the steep mountains would be difficult and expensive. So the people who lived along Lake Titicaca made their boats from a reed plant that grows in the lake. This reed is called balsa de totora. People made the boats by tying the balsa de totora together. They used the reeds to make floating wharves and piers that could support houses and storage buildings.

Ancient Egyptians also faced the challenge of making boats without wood. Egyptian boat builders used bundles of papyrus rushes tied together to build spindle-shaped barges. This same type of craft still sails on the Nile River today. When Egyptians needed larger boats to transport heavy loads, they imported tree trunks from Lebanon at great expense.

Above: A rock painting shows a dugout decorated with animal heads at both ends. Though the painting was found in the Sahara Desert, it dates back to a time long ago when rivers and lakes covered the land.

Above: A small silver model depicts an ancient Mesopotamian boat.

Left: A painting of a sailboat on an Egyptian vase is the oldest known drawing of a sailboat. The vase is 6,000 years old.

8

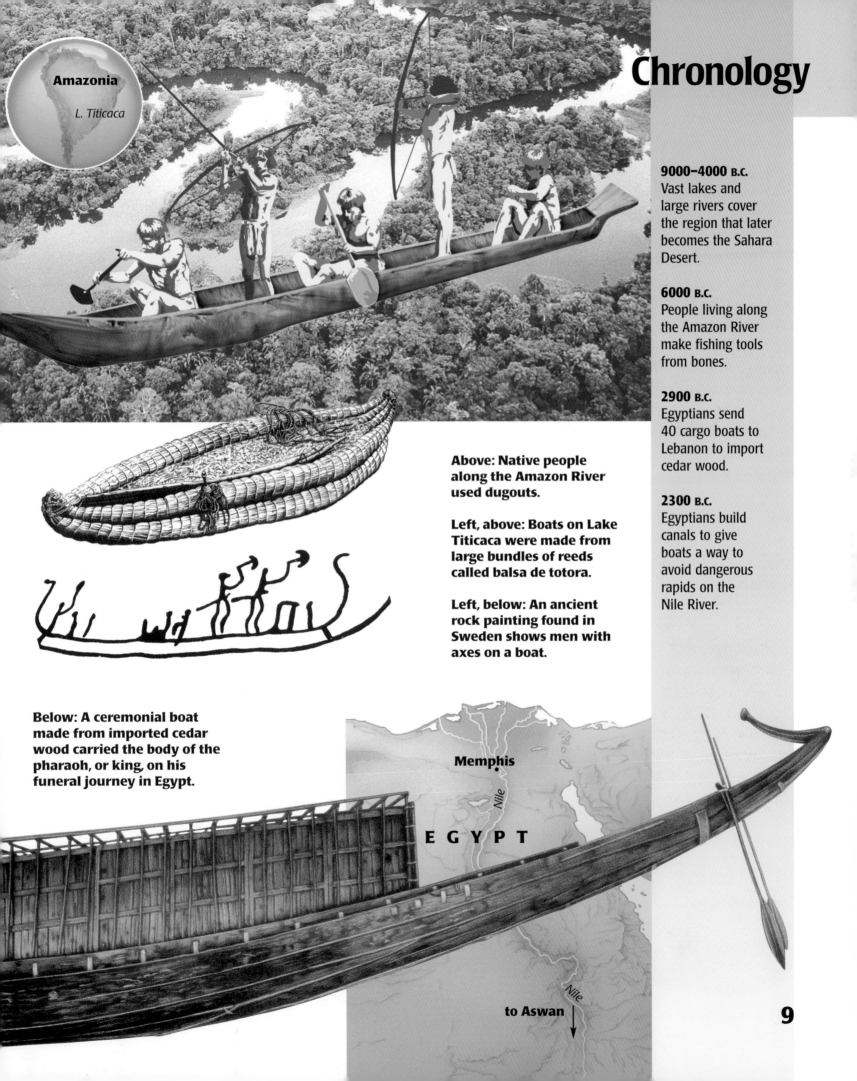

Amazonia

L. Titicaca

9000–4000 B.C.
Vast lakes and large rivers cover the region that later becomes the Sahara Desert.

6000 B.C.
People living along the Amazon River make fishing tools from bones.

2900 B.C.
Egyptians send 40 cargo boats to Lebanon to import cedar wood.

2300 B.C.
Egyptians build canals to give boats a way to avoid dangerous rapids on the Nile River.

Above: Native people along the Amazon River used dugouts.

Left, above: Boats on Lake Titicaca were made from large bundles of reeds called balsa de totora.

Left, below: An ancient rock painting found in Sweden shows men with axes on a boat.

Below: A ceremonial boat made from imported cedar wood carried the body of the pharaoh, or king, on his funeral journey in Egypt.

Memphis

Nile

E G Y P T

Nile

to Aswan

Canoes

Native American people found many ways to make boats that suited their needs. The Algonquian Indians, for example, found a way to make a boat called a canoe from tree bark. The Algonquian, who lived in the Ontario valley between the United States and Canada, were expert builders of these canoes. They made the frame of the boat with young trees, or saplings. They tied the saplings together with plant fibers. Then they covered the sapling frame with bark. They used the plant fibers to sew together strips of bark that had been collected from birch or elm trees. They used resin from spruce trees to make the bark waterproof. The canoes were strong but lightweight, so people could easily carry them around waterfalls or swamps. The Algonquian used their canoes for hunting, for fur trading, and for war.

Above: The Chono tribe on the coast of Tierra del Fuego in South America made a boat called a dalca from three planks of sturdy wood.

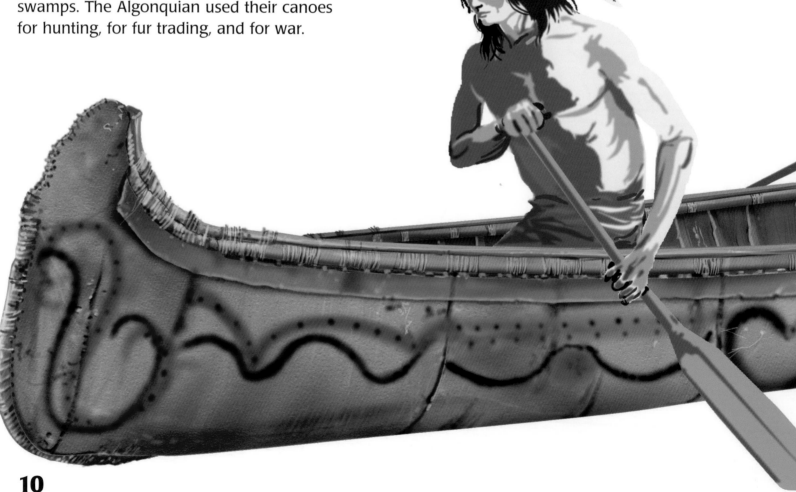

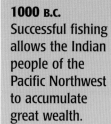

Above: The Chono, who used canoes like this one, were sometimes called canoeros (canoe people).

Above: The Algonquian made their canoes with tree bark.

1000 B.C.
Successful fishing allows the Indian people of the Pacific Northwest to accumulate great wealth.

1000 B.C.– A.D.1000
Groups migrate from Siberia to settle along the coasts of Alaska and Greenland.

Native American people who lived on the northwest coast of North America built a different kind of boat. On the Pacific Coast, people needed boats that were strong enough to take into the ocean and small enough to take into the local rivers. The Haida people, for example, made their boats by hollowing out tree trunks. They painted their dugouts with good luck symbols. Using their dugouts, the Haida people became expert in fishing in the ocean and in rivers. They caught large fish and whales from their dugout canoes.

The Inuit people in Alaska found still another way to make boats. Inuit used driftwood to make the frame of their long, narrow boat. They covered the frame with skins from caribou, deer, or seals. They called their boats kayaks and used them for hunting and fishing in Arctic waters.

Above: The Haida hunted in dugouts decorated with good luck symbols.

Right: Boats line the shore of a Haida village on the Pacific Coast of North America.

Below: Indians of the Pacific Northwest built boats to help them catch whales.

Below: The Inuit made kayaks using driftwood because there were no trees in the Arctic.

Gondolas of Venice

The gondola is one of the world's best-known boats. It is the symbol of the city of Venice, Italy, a city built on a lagoon. Many of Venice's streets are actually water-filled canals. The gondola's shape was designed with the city's narrow canals in mind. The craft is long and thin so it can pass through the canals. The bottom is flat to help it move through shallow waters without hitting bottom. The boat is not straight. It curves to the right. This shape helps the gondolier, who stands at the stern, or rear, of the craft to steer it alone and with just one oar. Only a portion of the prow, the front of the boat, and the stern touch the water. The shape makes the gondola easy to steer.

Above: The decoration on the prow, at the front end of the gondola, is called a ferro. No one knows how the ferro came to have its special shape. According to local legend, the ferro is said to resemble the shape of the hat worn by an ancient leader of Venice. The six prongs on the left are said to represent Venice's six city districts. The prong on the opposite side is said to represent the nearby lagoon city of Giudecca. No one really knows if these tales are true.

Below: A gondolier rows with a beech wood oar that rests on a forcola, a lock that holds the oar in place. The forcola is carved from a single piece of walnut wood. Its size depends on the height and weight of the gondolier.

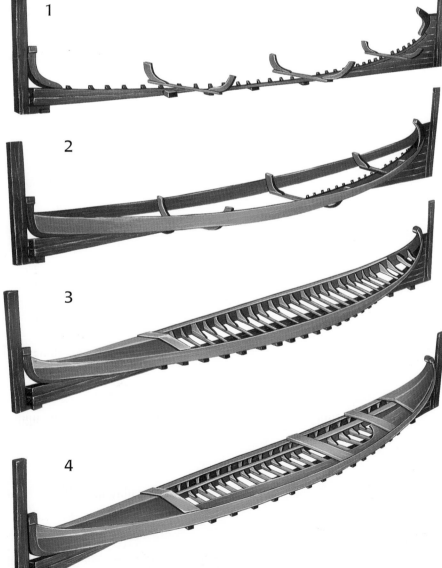

Right: The construction of the gondola follows traditional methods that have been used for centuries.

1) The first of the 280 pieces used to build the craft are assembled. They are placed in a way to form the prow, the stern, and the three main ribs of the gondola.

2) Oak planks, called cerchi, are added. To give the planks their curves, gondola makers soak them in water, bend them, and then dry them over a fire.

3) Thirty-three more ribs are added to the gondola.

4) Crosspieces reinforce the gondola, and planks are added to the bottom.

A.D. 810
People begin to live in the region later known as Venice.

13th century
First gondolas appear in Venice.

1300
A celebration called Fiesta della Sensa (Marriage with the Adriatic Sea) begins. It includes a gondola parade.

1562
Lawmakers think the gondolas are being decorated too much. They pass a law requiring the 10,000 gondolas in Venice to be painted black.

17th century
The ferro is added to the prow of the gondola.

Lifeboats

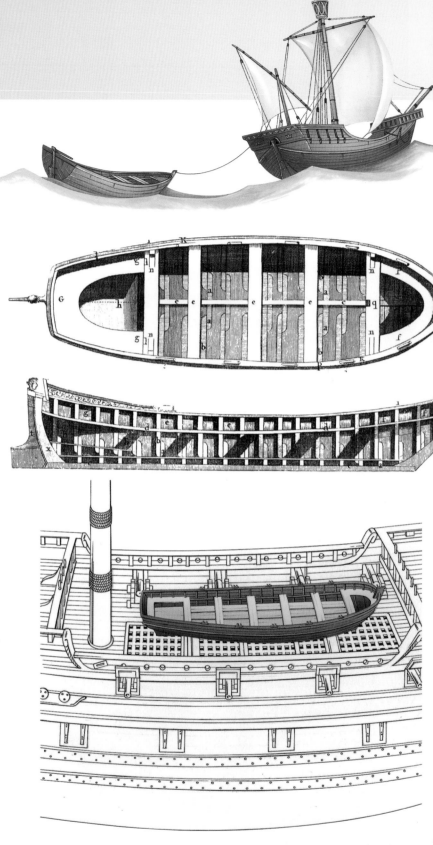

As early as the 14th century, ships in the Mediterranean Sea sailed with a line attached to another small boat called a launch. When the ships were at anchor, the launches took people to and from land. But the launches had another use. If a shipwreck occurred, the launches gave people a chance to survive.

The great steamships that later traveled on the oceans of the world carried lifeboats. But in 1912, when the *Titanic* sank in the Atlantic Ocean, it was carrying only enough lifeboats to hold about half of the passengers and crew members aboard. After 1,522 people died in the shipwreck, new rules required ships to carry enough lifeboats to hold everyone aboard.

Right, top: A carrack, the most common ship on the Mediterranean Sea in medieval times, sailed with a boat tied to the stern.

Right, center: Drawings show the top and cross-sectional views of a launch from an 18th-century ship.

Right: The launch on the deck of a 17th-century Dutch warship was used to take people to and from land when the ship was anchored.

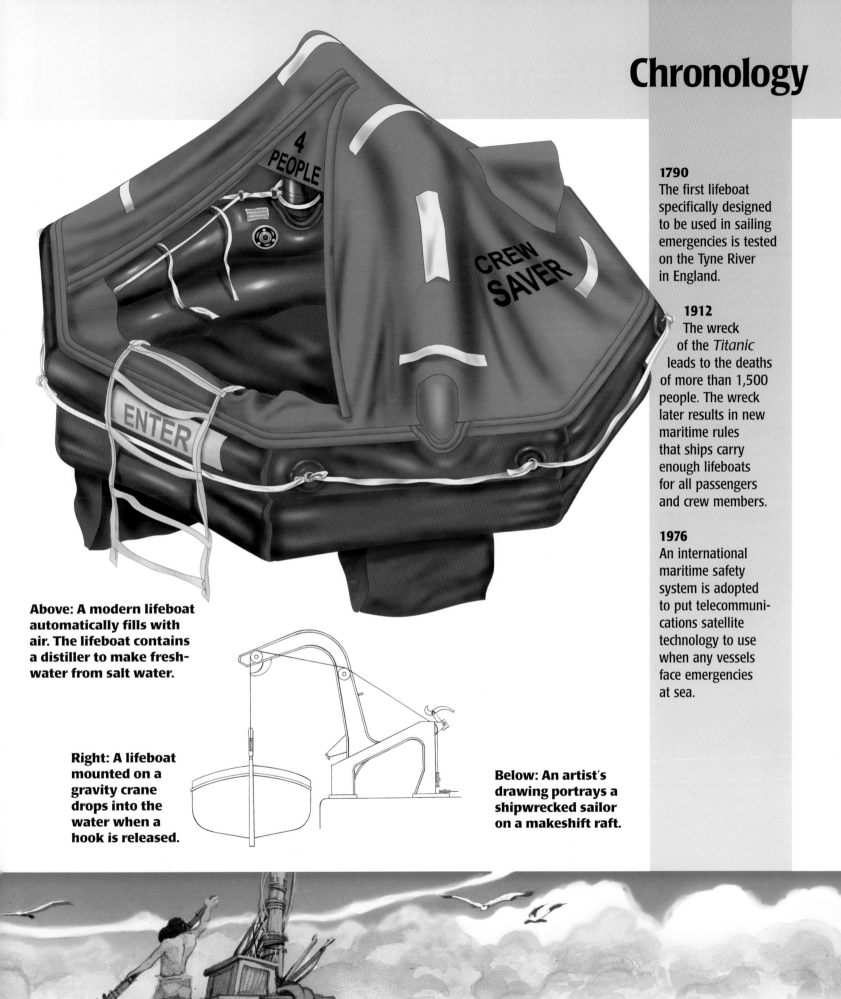

4 PEOPLE

CREW SAVER

ENTER

Above: A modern lifeboat automatically fills with air. The lifeboat contains a distiller to make freshwater from salt water.

Right: A lifeboat mounted on a gravity crane drops into the water when a hook is released.

Below: An artist's drawing portrays a shipwrecked sailor on a makeshift raft.

1790
The first lifeboat specifically designed to be used in sailing emergencies is tested on the Tyne River in England.

1912
The wreck of the *Titanic* leads to the deaths of more than 1,500 people. The wreck later results in new maritime rules that ships carry enough lifeboats for all passengers and crew members.

1976
An international maritime safety system is adopted to put telecommunications satellite technology to use when any vessels face emergencies at sea.

Moving Heavy Loads

Early civilizations in many parts of the world learned that one of the easiest ways to move heavy objects was by using waterways. In modern times, trucks transport freight on highways, and planes fly cargo through the skies. But the world still depends on barges traveling on rivers and on oceans to transport freight.

In ancient times, Egyptians used the Nile River as a water highway. Ships traveled the Nile transporting heavy loads. The tale of one famous barge journey still survives. Hatshepsut is believed to have ruled Egypt from 1473 to 1458 B.C. She was the first woman pharaoh of Egypt and built many structures. She imported giant obelisks, stone pillars, to adorn the temples of Luxor. Fragments of carvings from ancient Egypt show that the giant pillars traveled to the temples on a barge. About 30 boats towed the barge down the Nile River. Nearly 1,000 men rowed the boats.

Above: The English ship (right) and Indian freighter (left) were used in the 18th century on inland waterways. The Indian-style freighter is still in use.

Above: The people who built Stonehenge in England may have used platforms fastened to dugouts that had been lashed together to transport the stones from southern Wales.

Above: Though no one knows exactly how the Olmec people of Mexico moved giant stone heads to their communities, an artist's drawing shows one system they might have used. The Olmec could have brought the stones from distant quarries on waterways.

Left: A drawing shows the barge that brought two obelisks to Egypt for temples being built by the Egyptian pharaoh Hatshepsut.

Below: Horses pull a barge along a canal in France.

5000 B.C.
Rafts called keleks are used to transport heavy loads in Mesopotamia. Keleks are platforms attached to floats made of animal skins.

2250 B.C.
The people of Stonehenge begin transporting stones from Wales.

1473–1458 B.C.
Hatshepsut reigns as Egypt's first woman pharaoh.

1200–100 B.C.
The Olmec civilization thrives in Mexico.

7th century A.D.
China constructs the Great Canal. Men and animals use ropes to pull barges along the canal.

Voyages on the Open Sea

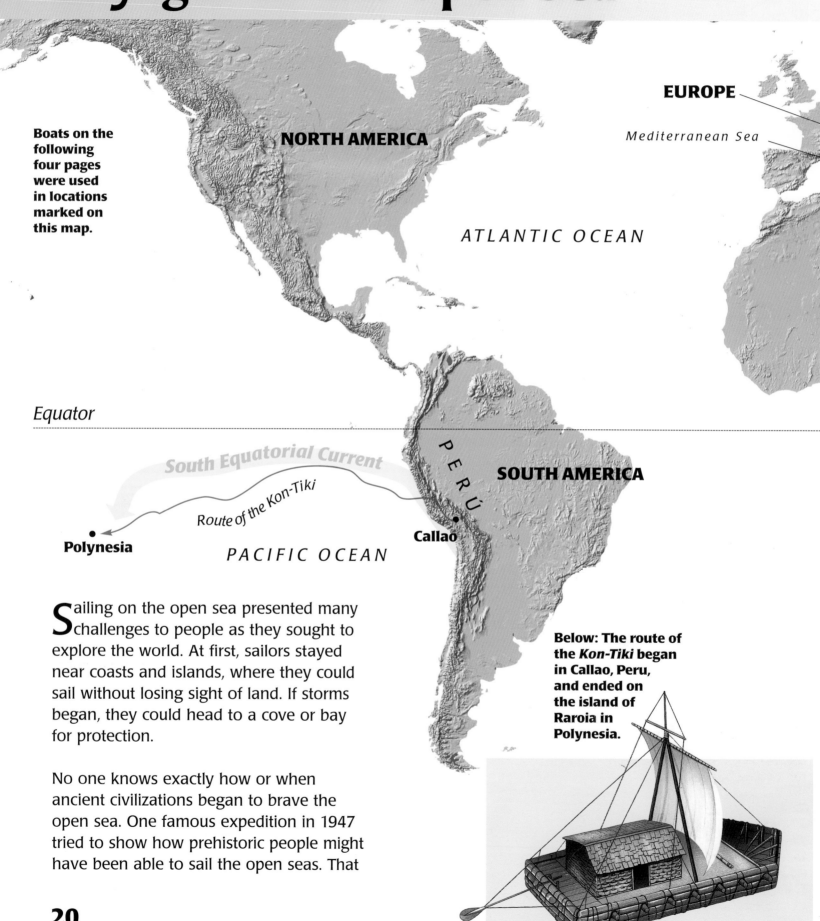

EUROPE

Mediterranean Sea

NORTH AMERICA

ATLANTIC OCEAN

Boats on the following four pages were used in locations marked on this map.

Equator

South Equatorial Current

P E R Ú

SOUTH AMERICA

Route of the Kon-Tiki

Polynesia

Callao

PACIFIC OCEAN

Sailing on the open sea presented many challenges to people as they sought to explore the world. At first, sailors stayed near coasts and islands, where they could sail without losing sight of land. If storms began, they could head to a cove or bay for protection.

No one knows exactly how or when ancient civilizations began to brave the open sea. One famous expedition in 1947 tried to show how prehistoric people might have been able to sail the open seas. That

Below: The route of the *Kon-Tiki* began in Callao, Peru, and ended on the island of Raroia in Polynesia.

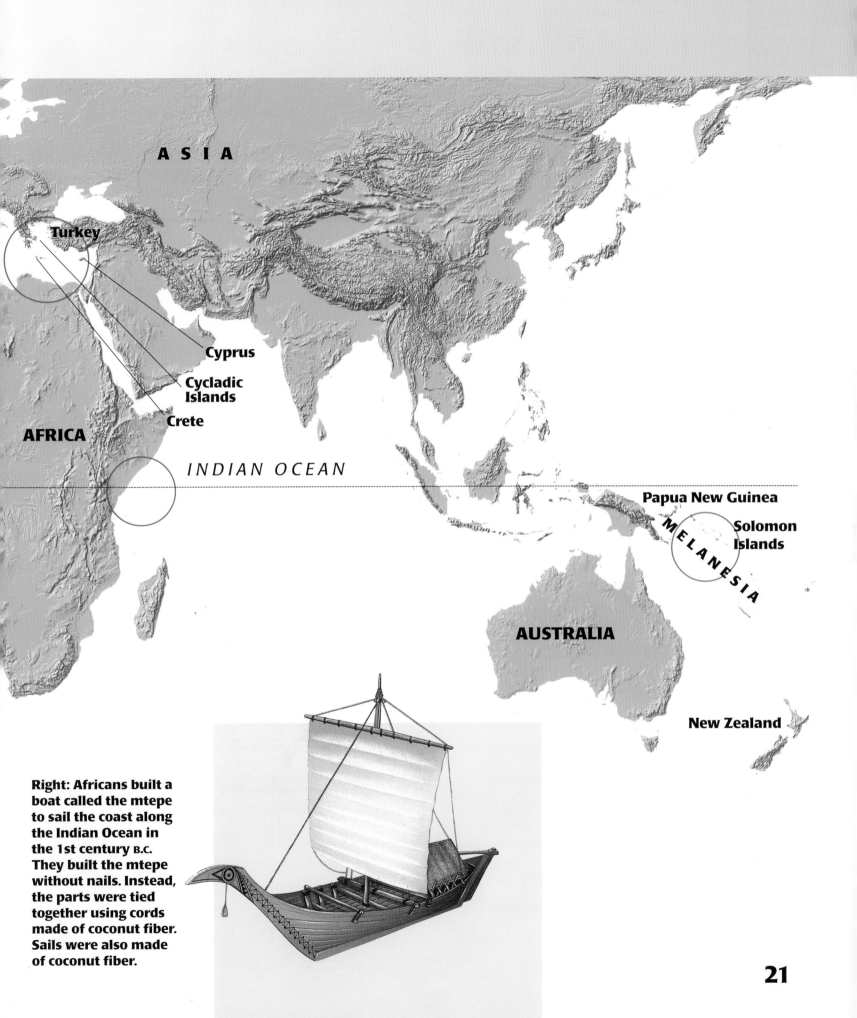

A S I A

Turkey

Cyprus

Cycladic
Islands

Crete

AFRICA

INDIAN OCEAN

Papua New Guinea

Solomon
Islands

M E L A N E S I A

AUSTRALIA

New Zealand

Right: Africans built a boat called the mtepe to sail the coast along the Indian Ocean in the 1st century B.C. They built the mtepe without nails. Instead, the parts were tied together using cords made of coconut fiber. Sails were also made of coconut fiber.

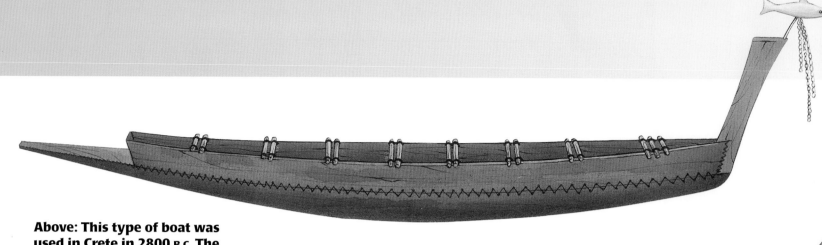

Above: This type of boat was used in Crete in 2800 B.C. The post on its stern is decorated with the figure of a fish.

year, a Norwegian explorer and writer named Thor Heyerdahl went on a voyage. He wanted to test his theory that prehistoric South Americans might have traveled to Polynesia in the South Pacific. He built a balsa wood raft that was a copy of a prehistoric South American design. The raft was made of nine balsa logs from Ecuador. Heyerdahl called the raft the *Kon-Tiki* after an Incan sun god. He and five crew members set sail from Peru on April 28, 1947.

On the journey, the crew ate only what they were able to catch in the Pacific Ocean. The only modern equipment they carried was a radio. Their journey lasted 101 days and covered 4,300 miles (6,920 km). They landed on the island of Raroia in Polynesia.

The journey did not convince all scientists that ancient South American civilizations had indeed made such a trip. But the expedition captured the public's imagination. The adventures of the *Kon-Tiki* led to a best-selling book and a documentary film that won an Academy Award. The *Kon-Tiki* is on display at a museum in Oslo, Norway.

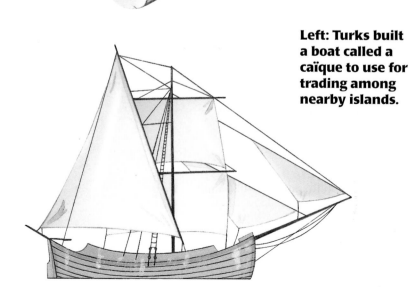

Left: Turks built a boat called a caïque to use for trading among nearby islands.

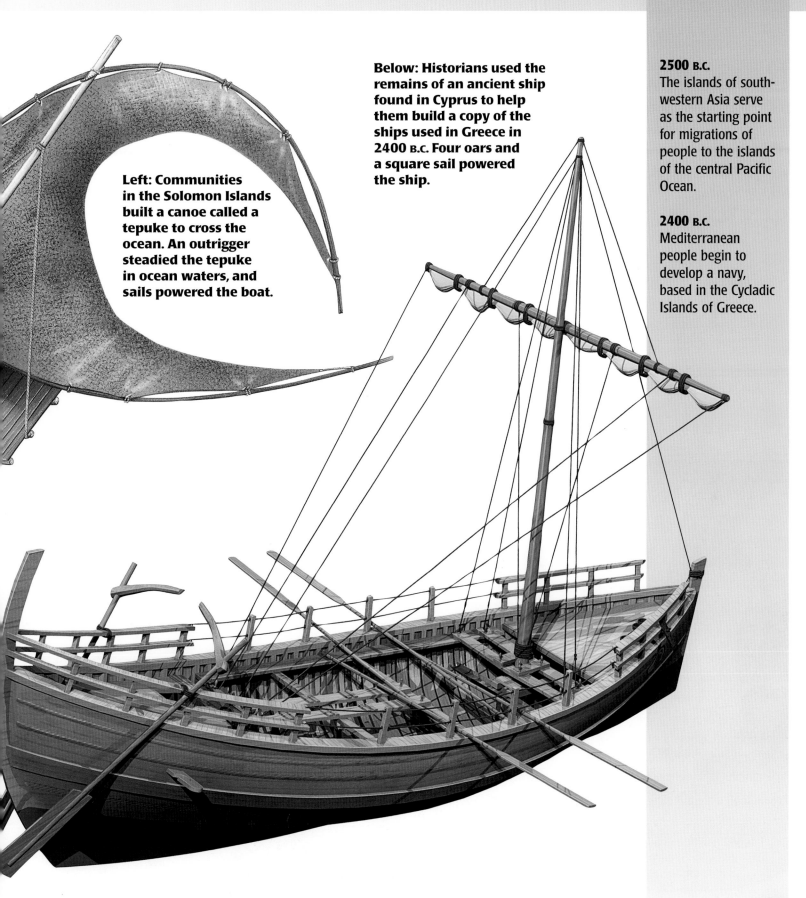

Below: Historians used the remains of an ancient ship found in Cyprus to help them build a copy of the ships used in Greece in 2400 B.C. Four oars and a square sail powered the ship.

Left: Communities in the Solomon Islands built a canoe called a tepuke to cross the ocean. An outrigger steadied the tepuke in ocean waters, and sails powered the boat.

2500 B.C.
The islands of southwestern Asia serve as the starting point for migrations of people to the islands of the central Pacific Ocean.

2400 B.C.
Mediterranean people begin to develop a navy, based in the Cycladic Islands of Greece.

Building Wooden Boats

Boatbuilding is among the oldest engineering pursuits. Modern boats and ships are built from aluminum and other man-made materials. But before these materials were created, boatbuilders usually relied upon wood. It was a logical choice. Wood floats, and in many places it is readily available. Also, it is possible to work with wood to make it into the shapes boatbuilders need. Boatbuilders usually steamed the wood to bend it into curved shapes. Builders used one piece of wood to form a boat's keel, the main structural piece that extends from one end to the other. They built the hull, or body, of the boat by adding ribs and planks that gave the vessel its shape.

Below: An image from an 11th-century tapestry shows Norman carpenters building boats.

Above: Planks used to build a boat are curved, depending on where on the boat they will be used.

2200 B.C.
Boat hulls are built without ribs. Pieces of wood often are joined with wooden pegs.

2000 B.C.
The steering oar, tied to the outside of the stern, appears on boats in Egypt.

2000–200 B.C.
Boats made of animal skins or wooden planks sewn or lashed together are used in northern Europe. Builders give the boats a rim that extends beyond the ends of the boat to provide handles for people to carry them ashore.

1500 B.C.
Keels are used on many types of boats in the Mediterranean Sea.

6th century B.C.
Boats with ribbed hulls are built in Corinth, Greece.

Right: Different hull shapes serve different purposes.

1) A flat-bottomed hull gives more space inside the boat. It is not as fast or seaworthy as other shapes.

2) A V-shaped hull is used for boats that need to be fast. Its shape helps the boat cut through the water.

3) The round-bottomed hull has more speed and seaworthiness than a flat-bottomed hull, and more interior space than a V-shaped hull.

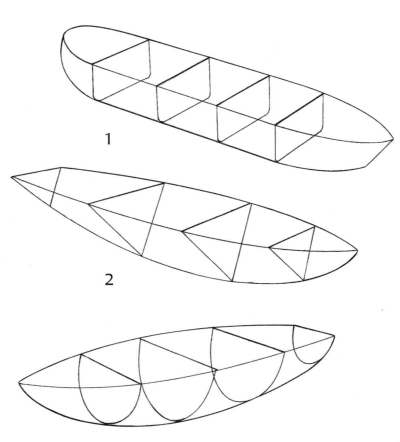

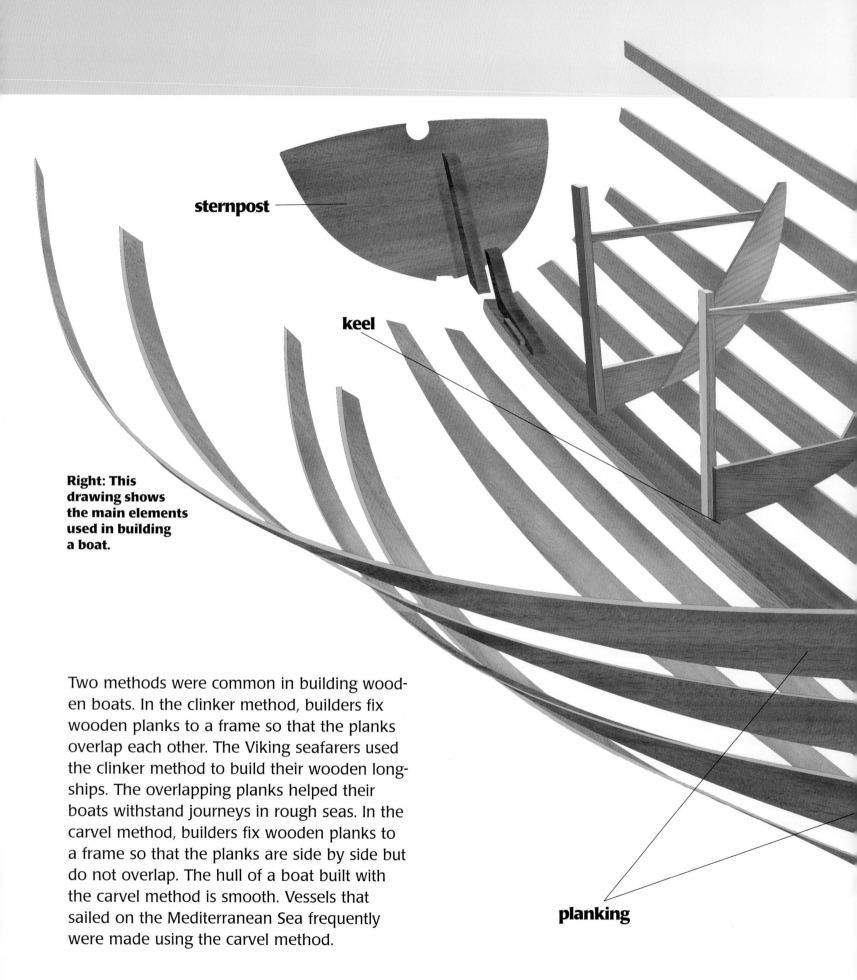

sternpost

keel

Right: This drawing shows the main elements used in building a boat.

planking

Two methods were common in building wooden boats. In the clinker method, builders fix wooden planks to a frame so that the planks overlap each other. The Viking seafarers used the clinker method to build their wooden longships. The overlapping planks helped their boats withstand journeys in rough seas. In the carvel method, builders fix wooden planks to a frame so that the planks are side by side but do not overlap. The hull of a boat built with the carvel method is smooth. Vessels that sailed on the Mediterranean Sea frequently were made using the carvel method.

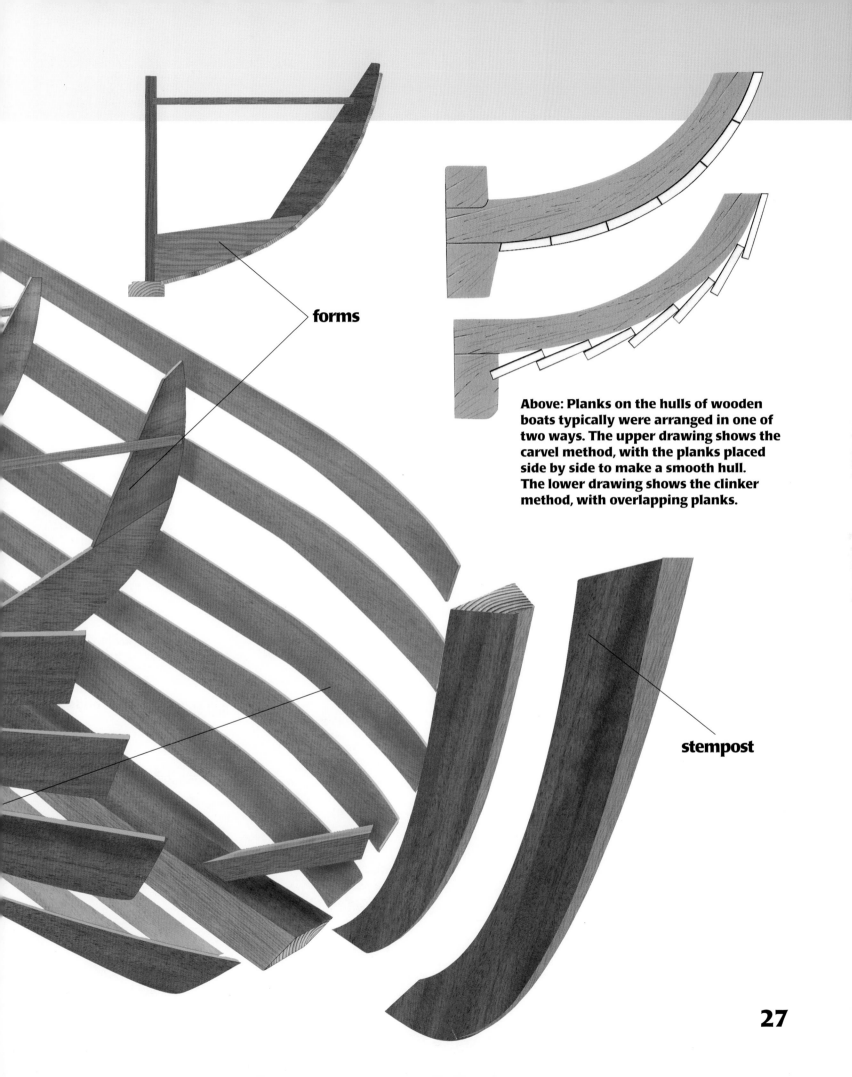

forms

Above: Planks on the hulls of wooden boats typically were arranged in one of two ways. The upper drawing shows the carvel method, with the planks placed side by side to make a smooth hull. The lower drawing shows the clinker method, with overlapping planks.

stempost

Sails

Sails allow boats to harness the wind. Historians believe that the first sails were made about 6,000 years ago. One period of history, roughly from 1560 until 1862, is known as the Age of Sail. The name comes from the important role that sailing ships played in war, trade, and migration at that time.

Two main types of sails are used on boats. Square sails use wind pressure to move the craft forward. Triangular or lateen sails act like a wing, using the wind to get a lifting action. They can be used to take advantage of winds coming from different directions. Sails hang on a pole called a yard or a mast. They are attached at the bottom to another pole called a boom. Sailors tighten or loosen ropes called sheets to keep the sails at a certain angle to the wind.

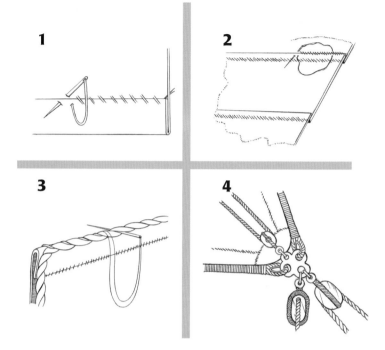

Above: Sails must be sewn and attached to ships. 1) A sail's hem is stitched. 2) Whipstitches join canvas panels of a sail. 3) Cording protects a sail's corners. 4) A patch reinforces the lower corner of a sail. A device called a grommet allows ropes to be attached.

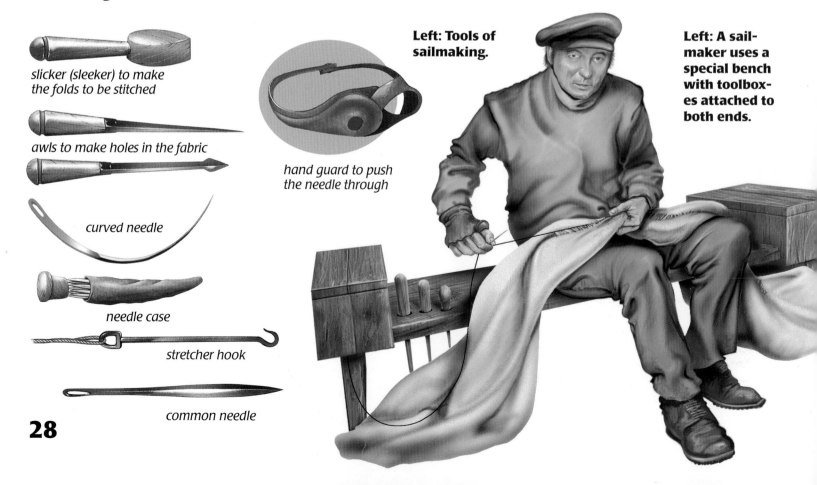

slicker (sleeker) to make the folds to be stitched

awls to make holes in the fabric

curved needle

needle case

stretcher hook

common needle

hand guard to push the needle through

Left: Tools of sailmaking.

Left: A sailmaker uses a special bench with toolboxes attached to both ends.

Right: The rigging of a sailing ship.

Below: Drawings show how rectangular canvas panels are sewn together to make a square sail (1) and a lateen sail (2). Spinnaker sails, with a curved top and bottom, may be made with canvas panels arranged horizontally (3), vertically (4), or horizontally along the bottom and in a fan shape above (5).

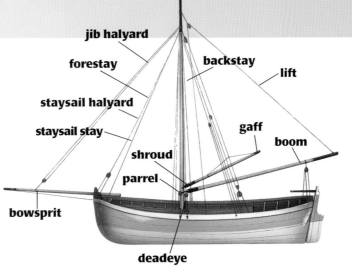

masthead · mast · jib halyard · forestay · backstay · lift · staysail halyard · gaff · staysail stay · boom · shroud · parrel · deadeye · bowsprit

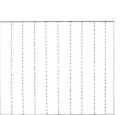

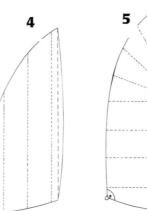

1

2

3

4

5

4000 B.C.
An artist paints a sail on an Egyptian vase. When found by archaeologists thousands of years later, the painting offers the first evidence of humans' use of sails.

2650 B.C.
A fleet of transport ships on the Nile River uses square linen sails.

2000 B.C.
Polynesian double canoes have palm leaf sails.

250 B.C.
Triangular or lateen sails appear in the Mediterranean Sea.

A.D. 1000
Chinese boats use sails made of straw mats reinforced by strips of bamboo.

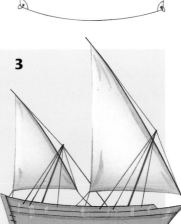

1

2

3

Drawings show basic types of sails. 1) The square sail, the oldest type of sail, is supported by a horizontal yard. 2) The lugsail is attached to a yard hung beneath the top of the mast. 3) The lateen sail is triangular in shape. 4) The spritsail is kept stretched by a diagonal pole called a sprit. The sprit fastens to the lower part of the mast. 5) The Marconi or Bermuda sail is a type of triangular sail often used on racing yachts.

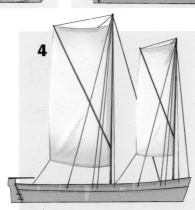

4

5

Fishing

For thousands of years, people have fished for food. People in ancient civilizations used large spears called harpoons with points made from horns or bones to capture their prey. Scientists who study ancient civilizations rely on tools, paintings, and other artworks that have survived to discover how people fished. Throughout the world, people found ways to use spears, nets, and traps to catch fish.

In modern times, fishing is a sport and an industry. People fish on rivers, lakes, and the ocean just for fun. Commercial fishing uses technology to help them find their prey much more quickly than once was possible. For example, fishing boats have sonar equipment, which uses sound waves to find fish. Many boats have processing factories on board to prepare the catch for sale.

Commercial fishing methods work so well that they are threatening the world's supply of some species of fish. People now worry that some fish will become extinct, or die out. Some restrictions are being placed on fishing to help certain species survive. For example, the loss of cod off the coast of Newfoundland led Canada to ban all cod fishing there in 1992. Five years later, when the cod population had grown, Canada allowed some limited cod fishing again.

Above: The scene created in an ancient African rock painting shows people in small boats fishing. They use harpoons and assegais, a type of spear.

Right: Wicker fish traps were used by ancient civilizations, and they are still used in many parts of the world. The drawing to the left of the trap shows how it works.

Below: Fishermen at Ingle Lake in Myanmar use traditional cone-shaped fish traps.

Chronology

Above: A model from an Egyptian tomb dating to 2000 B.C. shows fishing on the Nile River. Fishermen pull in the catch from a net stretched between two papyrus rafts.

Right: The jangada is a fishing boat that long has been used along the Brazilian coast. The jangada is a raft made of tree trunks and a hemp sail.

Right: A picture of fishing in New Guinea shows that age-old methods of fishing continue in modern times.

4000 B.C.
Egyptians fish in the Nile River and in swamps for a wide variety of fish, including the now extinct ossirinco.

2000 B.C.
Mesopotamian people venture into the Persian Gulf and Indian Ocean in search of fish.

A.D. 70
The Roman writer known as Pliny the Elder describes in his book *Natural History* the methods people use to catch fish.

10th century
Basque fishermen catch cod and whales in the Atlantic. They keep their best cod-fishing location, the waters off North America, a secret from their fishing competitors.

Fishing Boats

People have invented a variety of boats and tools to catch fish. Fishing boats usually traveled looking for schools of fish. Then crews would catch fish using lines, nets, or spears. To catch lobster or crab, fishing boats would drop lobster pots or baskets into the water.

One type of fishing boat that was used off the Newfoundland coast was called a dory. The dory is a small, flat-bottomed boat with a square sail. In the Mediterranean, fishing crews use a boat with a passerella, or catwalk, a long narrow walkway extending off the main boat. A crew member with a harpoon stands on the passerella, waiting for fish to appear below.

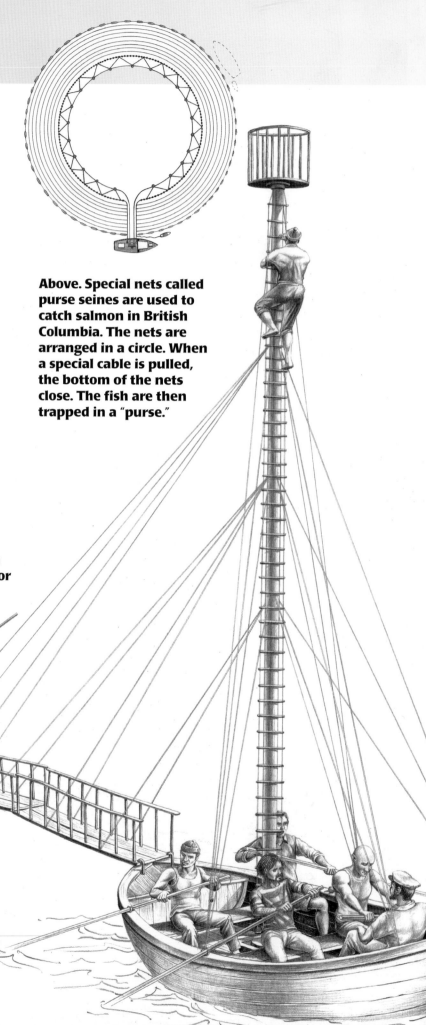

Above. Special nets called purse seines are used to catch salmon in British Columbia. The nets are arranged in a circle. When a special cable is pulled, the bottom of the nets close. The fish are then trapped in a "purse."

Right: A man on a passerella, or catwalk, holds his harpoon in hand to catch a swordfish. From the mast, the lookout watches for fish and tells the crew where to row to come closer to them.

Above: A drawing shows a fishing boat from Iceland.

Chronology

Left: Whaling boats needed six men to row the boat. When the boat drew close enough to the whale, the oarsman in front exchanged his oar for a harpoon tied to a line.

Below: Small dories had two-person crews. Dory fishers threw out setlines, long floating lines with many baited hooks attached. When full with cod, the dory took its load to a main ship and then went out to catch another load.

Below: Crews fishing for sardines, anchovies, and mackerel work at night. They use lights to attract schools of fish.

15th century
The prized fishing grounds that Basque fishing crews had tried to keep secret are discovered. Fishing boats from all over Europe flock to the Grand Banks of Newfoundland.

1946
The International Whaling Commission is created in Washington, D.C., to limit whale hunting.

1986
Greenpeace, an international group that tries to protect endangered species, begins protests against whale hunting.

1992
With the cod population rapidly declining, the Canadian government closes the waters of Newfoundland and the Grand Banks to fishing.

Boats from Asian and Arab Worlds

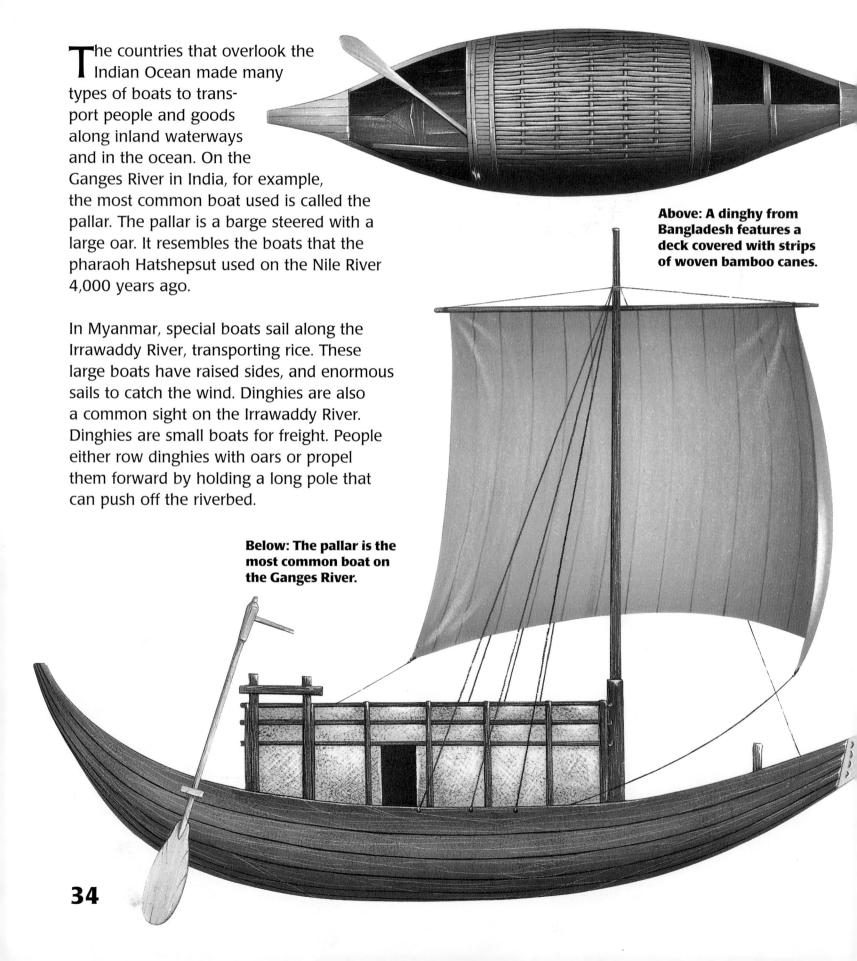

The countries that overlook the Indian Ocean made many types of boats to transport people and goods along inland waterways and in the ocean. On the Ganges River in India, for example, the most common boat used is called the pallar. The pallar is a barge steered with a large oar. It resembles the boats that the pharaoh Hatshepsut used on the Nile River 4,000 years ago.

In Myanmar, special boats sail along the Irrawaddy River, transporting rice. These large boats have raised sides, and enormous sails to catch the wind. Dinghies are also a common sight on the Irrawaddy River. Dinghies are small boats for freight. People either row dinghies with oars or propel them forward by holding a long pole that can push off the riverbed.

Above: A dinghy from Bangladesh features a deck covered with strips of woven bamboo canes.

Below: The pallar is the most common boat on the Ganges River.

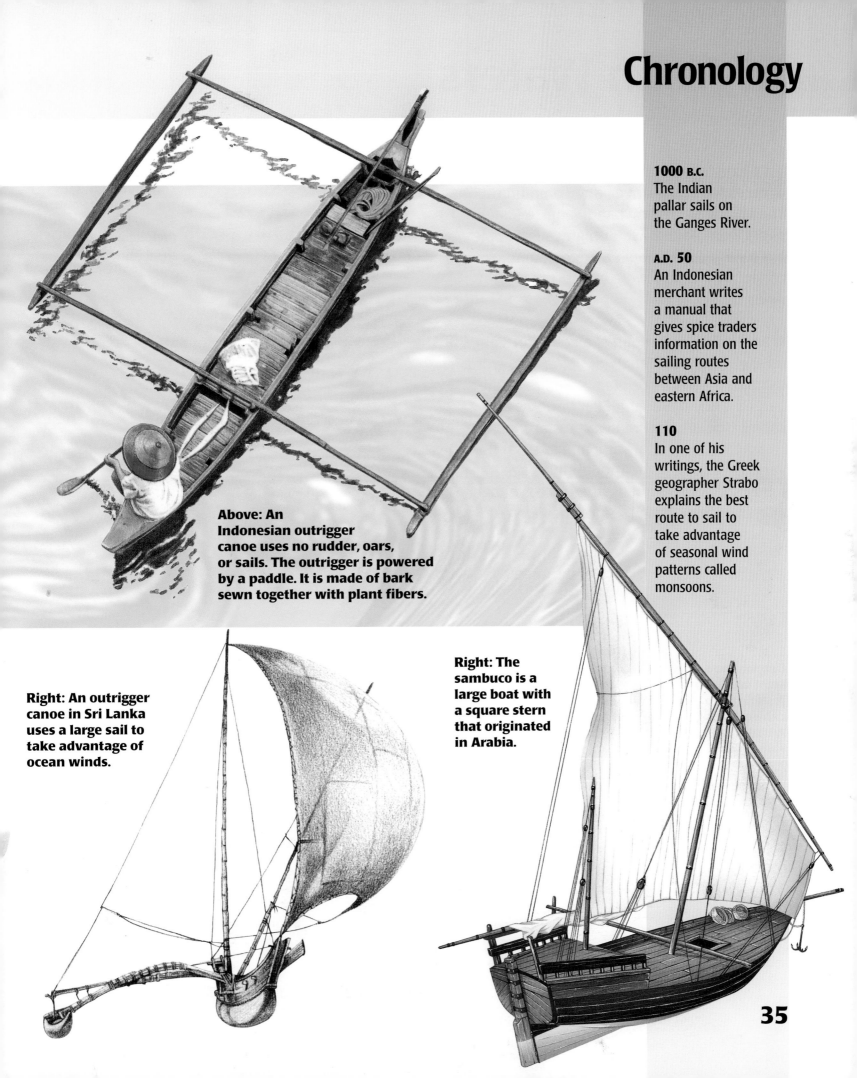

1000 B.C.
The Indian pallar sails on the Ganges River.

A.D. 50
An Indonesian merchant writes a manual that gives spice traders information on the sailing routes between Asia and eastern Africa.

110
In one of his writings, the Greek geographer Strabo explains the best route to sail to take advantage of seasonal wind patterns called monsoons.

Above: An Indonesian outrigger canoe uses no rudder, oars, or sails. The outrigger is powered by a paddle. It is made of bark sewn together with plant fibers.

Right: An outrigger canoe in Sri Lanka uses a large sail to take advantage of ocean winds.

Right: The sambuco is a large boat with a square stern that originated in Arabia.

35

In Asian Waters

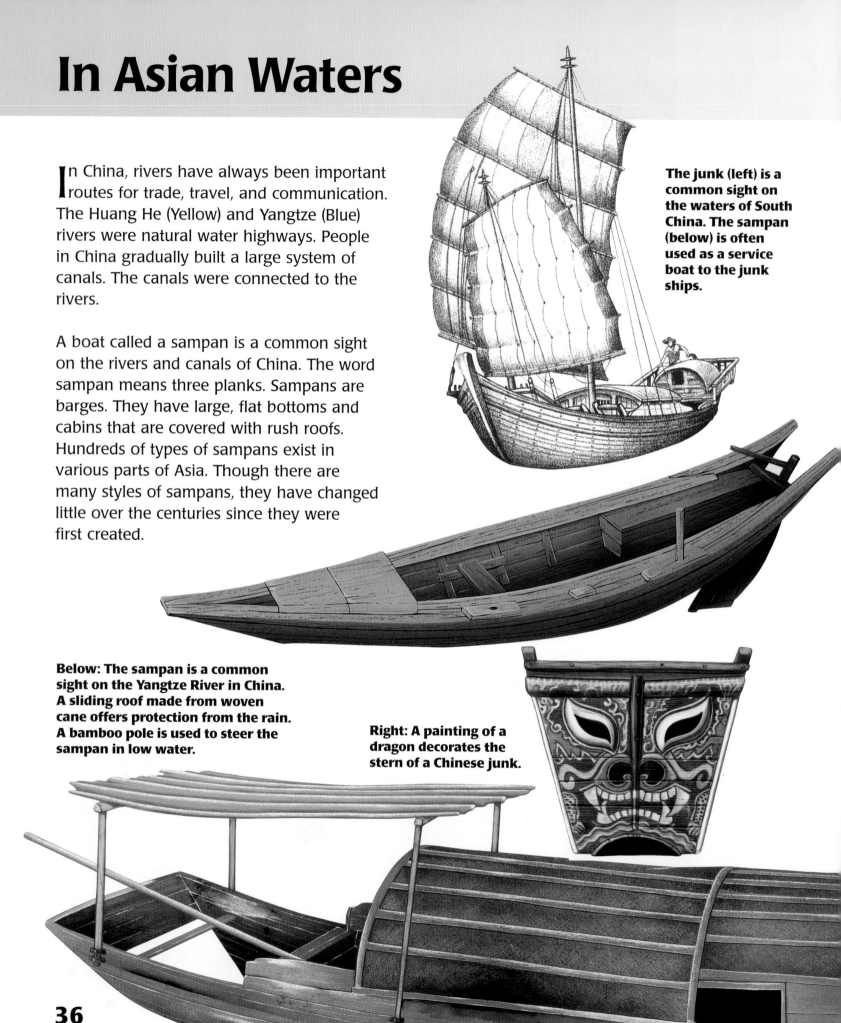

In China, rivers have always been important routes for trade, travel, and communication. The Huang He (Yellow) and Yangtze (Blue) rivers were natural water highways. People in China gradually built a large system of canals. The canals were connected to the rivers.

A boat called a sampan is a common sight on the rivers and canals of China. The word sampan means three planks. Sampans are barges. They have large, flat bottoms and cabins that are covered with rush roofs. Hundreds of types of sampans exist in various parts of Asia. Though there are many styles of sampans, they have changed little over the centuries since they were first created.

The junk (left) is a common sight on the waters of South China. The sampan (below) is often used as a service boat to the junk ships.

Below: The sampan is a common sight on the Yangtze River in China. A sliding roof made from woven cane offers protection from the rain. A bamboo pole is used to steer the sampan in low water.

Right: A painting of a dragon decorates the stern of a Chinese junk.

36

Chronology

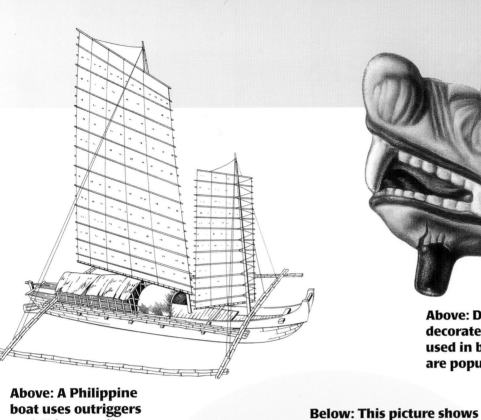

Above: A Philippine boat uses outriggers and Chinese sails.

Above: Dragon heads often decorate the prows of boats used in boat races, which are popular events in China.

Below: This picture shows a model of a boat that was used in Japan during the 6th and 7th centuries A.D. to reach the coasts of Korea and China.

Above: A 16th-century painting shows a Portuguese explorer with African slaves aboard a Japanese boat.

3rd century B.C.
China constructs the Magic Canal, the first waterway of its kind in the world. Chinese crews connected two rivers flowing in opposite directions with a canal that used hillsides to help channel the water.

A.D. 610
The Chinese build the Grand Canal joining the Huang He (Yellow) and Yangtze (Blue) rivers.

10th century
To permit boats to pass from one level of water to another, China begins using a sluice, a system to flood water from one level into another when needed.

1327
Work to extend the Grand Canal brings it to its final length of 1,056 miles (1,700 km).

Polynesian Explorers

The ancient Polynesian people explored and settled on islands in the South Pacific Ocean. They managed to travel long distances on seemingly fragile boats. Their lightweight canoes carried people, animals, plants, and supplies from one island to another.

Ancient Polynesians carved their boats using tools made from bones or coral. The boats may have seemed delicate, but the Polynesians found ways to make them strong enough to withstand rough ocean waters and to carry heavy loads. The Polynesians built many types of boats, and almost all of them used outriggers or more than one hull to give the boat more stability. They built platforms over the hulls to give them enough room to carry what they needed.

Right: An ancient rock drawing on Easter Island depicts a canoe.

Polynesians traveled without using a compass. They used their observations of the stars, the sun, the wind, and the ocean's currents to steer their course. They also used a matang, a nautical chart or map made of sticks, shells, and plant fibers. They devised clever ways to find islands while traveling vast ocean waters. Some crews carried a bird aboard and set it free occasionally. If the bird did not return to the boat, they knew it had found land. They then steered their boat in the direction of the bird's flight.

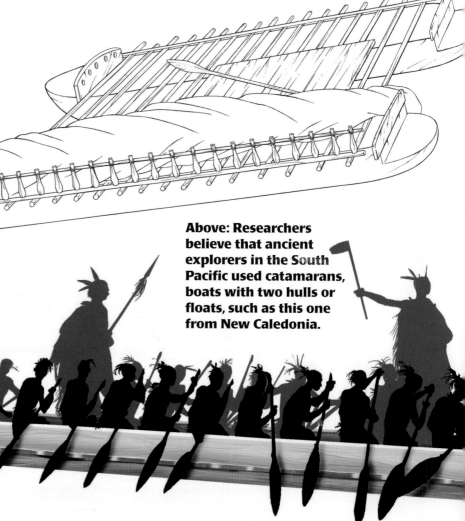

Below: Men using paddles powered the long, narrow waka taua, as the New Zealand war canoe was called.

Above: Researchers believe that ancient explorers in the South Pacific used catamarans, boats with two hulls or floats, such as this one from New Caledonia.

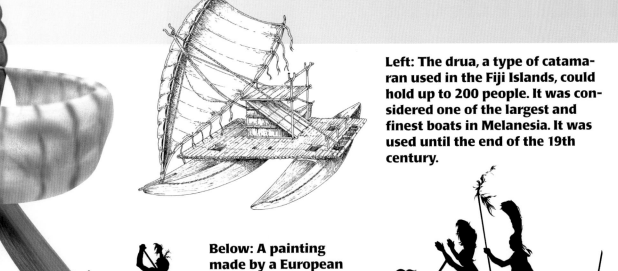

Left: The drua, a type of catamaran used in the Fiji Islands, could hold up to 200 people. It was considered one of the largest and finest boats in Melanesia. It was used until the end of the 19th century.

Below: A painting made by a European explorer in 1767 shows a Tahitian boat.

Left: A matang from the Marshall Islands in Micronesia uses shells to indicate islands' locations. Rods show how long the trip takes, depending on the currents and condition of the waves.

3000 B.C.
People from Southeast Asia migrate toward the Pacific islands.

1500 B.C.
Polynesian people settle in New Guinea and the Bismarck Archipelago.

1400 B.C.
Migrant settlers arrive in the Fiji Islands.

1300 B.C.
Tonga is settled.

1000 B.C.
Samoa is settled.

A.D. 300
Polynesians from Samoa explore the Marquesas Islands, Hawaii, New Zealand, and Easter Island.

Life on the Water

Boats are used for fishing, for travel, and to transport goods. In many parts of the world, boats are also places to live. There is a wide range of houseboats. Some simple boats are homes for poor people and immigrant refugees arriving in crowded, modern cities. Some floating houses are used by middle-class people. Other houseboats are luxurious. They are traveling homes for wealthy people.

In modern Hong Kong and in Bangkok, poor people live and work on small, flat-bottomed boats. In Amsterdam, floating houses line many city canals. The boats, which are permanently anchored, have street addresses. Seattle has about 500 side-by-side houseboats on Lake Union. Long ago, Seattle's neighborhoods on the water provided living quarters for loggers and fishers who wanted to live near their work. But now some of those quarters are floating mansions.

Right: Many poor people live on the Sarasvati River in India in homemade houseboats like this one.

40

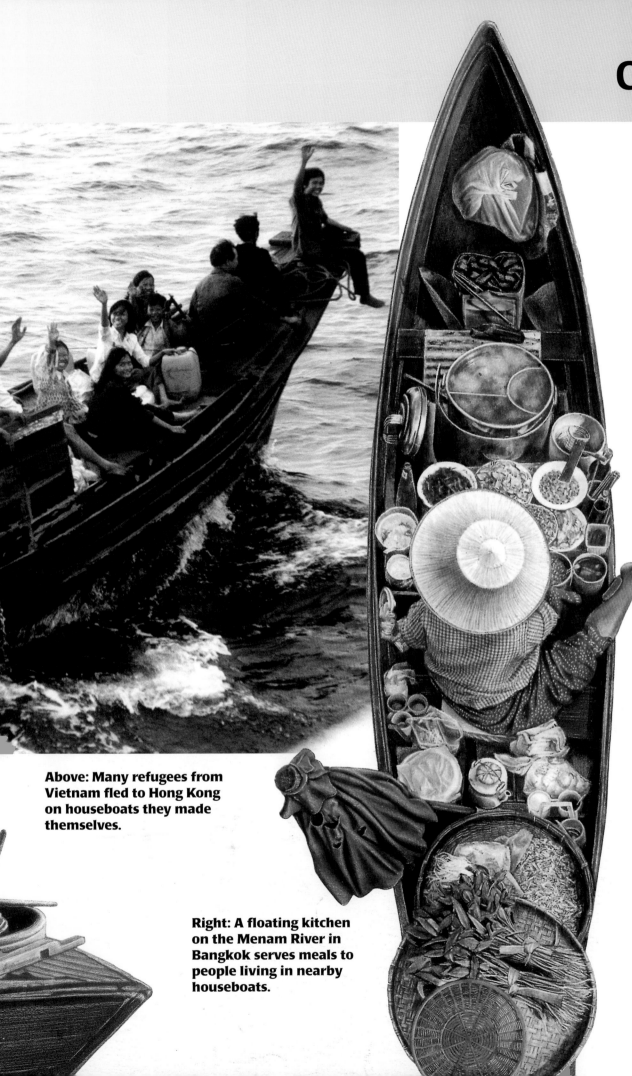

1874
Artist Claude Monet outfits a boat as a studio so he can work while on the Seine River.

1940s
The houseboat community in Seattle reaches its peak with about 2,000 houseboats on Lake Union.

1997
In Amsterdam, the *Hendrika Maria*, a barge that was used to transport gravel and coal before becoming a house-boat, is turned into the world's first houseboat museum.

Above: Many refugees from Vietnam fled to Hong Kong on houseboats they made themselves.

Right: A floating kitchen on the Menam River in Bangkok serves meals to people living in nearby houseboats.

Fun on the Water

Boats on the world's oceans, rivers, and lakes do many kinds of work, but some were invented just for fun. The sailboard, or windsurfer, is one example of a watercraft that is for recreation. In the summer of 1964, Newman Darby created an unusual boat for his girlfriend. The boat allowed her to sail while standing up and to control the boat without using a rudder. Darby's boat evolved into a board with a sail. A surfer and a sailor later combined their talents to refine Darby's invention. The key to the sailboard was a special kind of joint that kept the wind from lifting the sail off the board and allowed the surfer to use his or her weight to hold it in place. Windsurfing went on to become an Olympic sport and a multimillion-dollar industry.

Many other vehicles have been created for recreation. Pedal boats have bicycle pedals that turn a propeller to power the boat. Certain kinds of small rubber boats, called dinghies, are used on rivers by people on trips to enjoy the outdoors. They are good for what is called whitewater rafting because they can be steered through the white water of rapids on rivers.

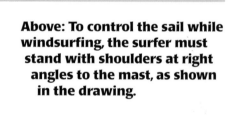

Above: To control the sail while windsurfing, the surfer must stand with shoulders at right angles to the mast, as shown in the drawing.

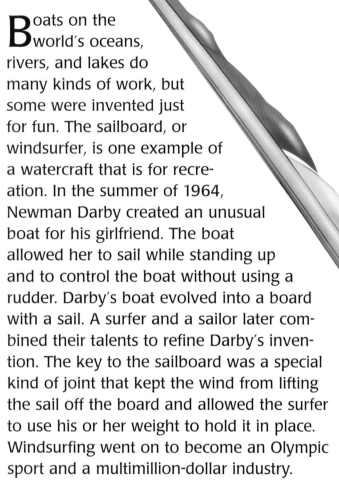

Right: Windsurfing combines sailing and surfing.

Right:
A fiberglass
pedal boat has
pedals for two people.

Above: This drawing shows how a pedal boat works. People power the boats by pedaling as if they were on a bicycle. Axles and gears attach the pedals to the boat's propeller.

A rubber dinghy can be propelled with oars (above) in calm water and with paddles (left) on river rapids.

1720
The first yacht club is founded in Cork, Ireland.

1829
For the first time, crews from the universities at Oxford and Cambridge compete in a boat race on the Thames River.

1968
In California, a sailor and a surfer receive a patent for the first sailboard.

1984
Windsurfing becomes an Olympic sport.

Water Races

Almost wherever there is water, there are water races. The America's Cup, a race among the world's fastest yachts, is one of the best-known examples. It is also one of the oldest sailing races in the world. The silver cup that goes to the winner has been called the oldest trophy in sport. The first race was held in 1851. A schooner called *America* represented the New York Yacht Club. Fifteen other sailing yachts represented the Royal Yacht Squadron in Great Britain. The yachts sailed around the Isle of Wight off the coast of England. America won by twenty minutes.

The modern America's Cup race is held every four years in different parts of the world. The number of boats in the competition varies. The winner of the cup competes to keep it against challengers who want to win the trophy.

Right: Two sailing yachts dueled in the Pacific Ocean off the coast of San Diego, California, in the 1992 America's Cup race.

Right: A kayaker steers through a whitewater course.

44

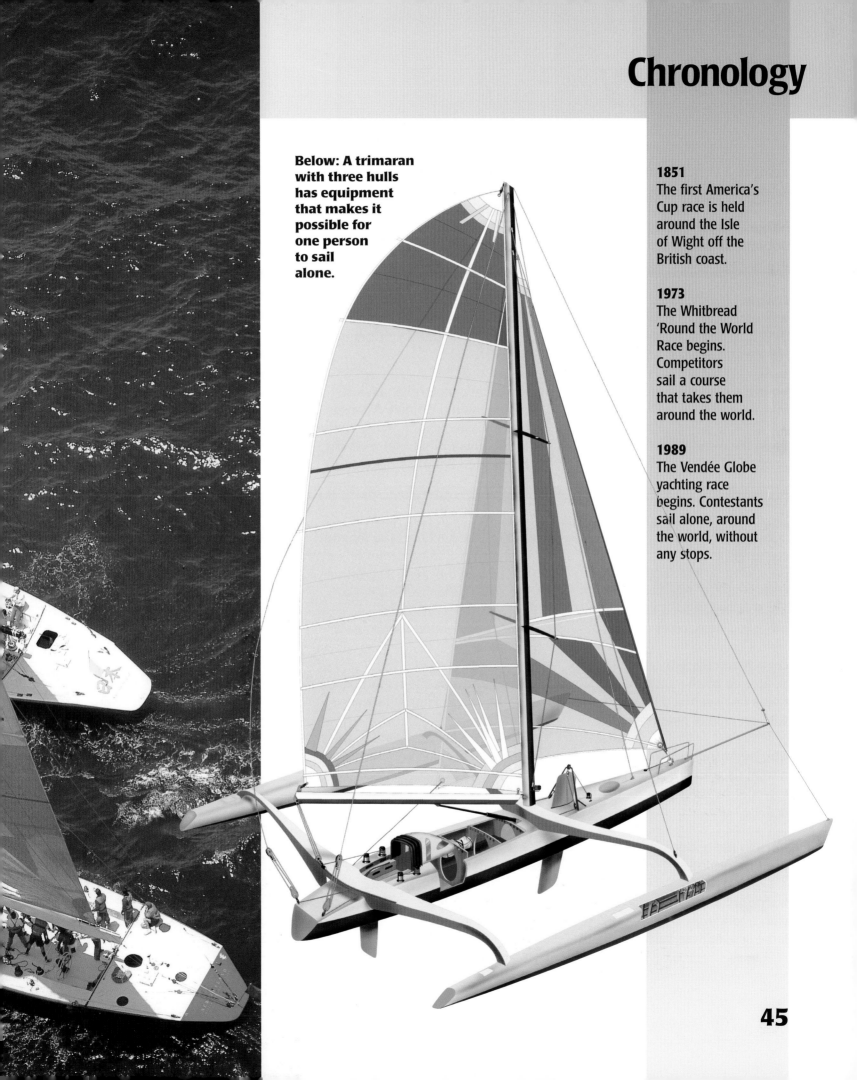

Below: A trimaran with three hulls has equipment that makes it possible for one person to sail alone.

1851
The first America's Cup race is held around the Isle of Wight off the British coast.

1973
The Whitbread 'Round the World Race begins. Competitors sail a course that takes them around the world.

1989
The Vendée Globe yachting race begins. Contestants sail alone, around the world, without any stops.

Glossary

assegai: a slender hardwood spear used in southern Africa.

barge: a large, usually flat-bottomed boat used to transport goods.

Basque: people living in the western Pyrenees near the Bay of Biscay on the border between France and Spain.

boom: a pole used to hold the bottom part of a sail.

bow: the front part of a boat or ship.

caïque: a light sailing vessel used in the eastern Mediterranean Sea region.

catamaran: a boat with two parallel hulls that support a flat surface above. Can also refer to a raft of logs lashed together and propelled by paddles or sails.

coracle or curragh: a small round boat used by the ancient Irish. It was made by covering a wicker frame with an animal hide or leather.

dinghy: a small open boat. Also a term used for an East Indian rowboat or sailboat. A rubber dinghy is a life raft.

dory: a flat-bottomed rowing boat used for fishing.

harpoon: a barbed spear or javelin with a long rope used in hunting large sea animals such as whales.

hemp: a tall Asian herb whose fibers can be used to make cords.

hoist: to raise or haul up, sometimes with a mechanical device.

hull: the body of a boat.

junk: a flat-bottomed boat with a square sail that is commonplace in China.

kayak: a canoe originally used by the Eskimo or Inuit. A kayak has a small opening in the center for one person, who propels the kayak with a double-bladed paddle.

keel: the main structural part of a ship. The keel runs the length of the ship along a center line from the bow to the stern. The frame of the ship is attached to the keel.

maritime: related to the sea or shipping.

Mesopotamia: the region between the Tigris and Euphrates rivers.

monsoon: periodic wind in the Indian Ocean and southern Asia. In the cold season the monsoon blows from land to sea, and in the hot season it blows from sea to land.

oar: a long pole with a wide, flat blade at one end, used for rowing.

obelisk: an upright, four-sided stone pillar.

Olmec: a civilization that lived in Central Mexico between 1500 B.C. and the 10th century A.D.

outrigger: a long, thin float attached parallel to a canoe by beams. The outrigger design helps make canoes more stable in rough waters.

paddle: a short pole with a wide, flat blade at one or both ends. It is not held in place like an oar.

Paleolithic age: a period of time roughly from 2.5 million years ago to about 12,000 years ago, when people began using some stone tools.

papyrus: a grasslike plant that grows in or near water, including the Nile River.

prow: the front part of a ship or boat.

rush: a plant with a long, hollow stem that grows in or near water.

sluice: a passage for water with an opening that allows the flow of water to be regulated.

stern: the rear part of a ship or boat.

whitewater rafting: a sport in which participants travel on a raft through a river where, in some places, the water moves fast enough to create a white, frothy foam.

For More Information

Nick Cook, *The World's Fastest Boats*.
Mankato, MN: Capstone Press, 2001.

Stephen Currie, *Thar She Blows: American
Whaling in the Nineteenth Century*. Minneapolis, MN:
Lerner, 2001.

James P. Delgado. *Native American Shipwrecks*.
New York: Franklin Watts, 2000.

Christin Ditchfield, *Kayaking, Canoeing, Rowing,
and Yachting*. New York: Childrens Press, 2000.

Charla L. Draper, *Cooking on Nineteenth-Century
Whaling Ships*. Mankato, MN: Blue Earth, 2001.

Eric Kentley, *Boat*. New York: Dorling Kindersley,
2000.

Arlene Bourgeois Molzahn, *Ships and Boats*.
Berkeley Heights, NJ: Enslow, 2003.

James Prosek, *A Good Day's Fishing*.
New York: Simon & Schuster, 2004.

Laura Purdie Salas, *Saltwater Fishing*.
Mankato, MN: Capstone Press, 2004.

Lola M. Schaefer, *Barges*. Mankato, MN:
Bridgestone, 2000.

Philip Wilkinson, *Ships*. New York:
Kingfisher, 2000.

Index